Summer
Haikai

Loss, Healing, and the Art of Gratitude

Claire V. Flaherty

PAGE PUBLISHING, INC.
Conneaut Lake, PA

First originally published by Page Publishing 2021

ISBN 978-1-6624-6400-3 (pbk)
ISBN 978-1-6624-1557-9 (hc)
ISBN 978-1-6624-1556-2 (digital)

Printed in the United States of America

For my brothers, dwelling without and dwelling within.

Contents

Introduction

The sixth of nine siblings, I enjoyed the rough and tumble childhood of a tagalong tomboy who hero-worshipped her three older brothers. In the era of Lionel trains and gas engine planes, I never imagined the day would come when I would outlive the older two. But I have. Insulated in the nineteenth century farmhouse that has long been sanctuary to me, I wanted an approach to maintaining momentum away from the pain of loss toward acceptance and the joy of life. Dawn had always been my favorite time of day when I felt most alive and at peace with the world. On the first day of summer, I determined to recapture it—away from midnight oil and morning meetings. Recovery from loss had always come to me through the simplicity of nature, and this time was no different. Having little talent with a brush but an eye for color and balance, the medium of juxtaposition I chose to accompany my haiku was the photographic image. There would be no greater elixir than my farmhouse garden, neighboring hillsides, and waterways—no stronger expression of life's beauty than the aesthetics of haikai.

June 21

Summer Haikai

I will not mourn you
on this first morn of Summer.
Look! Listen! Respire.

June 22

Outpouring

Breezes and shadows
comfort my settling in,
'til rains drive me out.

June 23

Diminutive

Lilies fold in prayer
unaware Olinis blooms
boldly greet the dawn.

June 24

Portals

The fenestrated
skyline rolls lazily by
through roses and pines.

June 25

Crepuscular

Like a pillow fight
choreographed in the clouds—
first light is a sound.

June 26

Wild Strawberries

Avian ambrosia—
succulent, luscious red orbs
beget morn arias.

June 27

Picea Pungens

Garden matriarch—
daemon of Christmas childhood,
destiny's blue thread.

June 28

Unrequited Love

Hope recedes as blooms
blanched by sun, rain, and time yield
to the setting sun.

June 29

Ode to Herman Hesse

Iris! Gertrude! All
anima! Eternity
my only rival.

June 30

Reminiscing

Cool salutations
stem July's tide, yet, only
for another day.

July 1

Morning Dew

Refrigeration
took its inspiration from
mornings such as these!

July 2

Donegal Springs

Through the stones sunward—
arctic life force courses down
toward parched roots and shoots.

July 3

Sunday Doldrums

Verses elude me—
like the fragrance of honey
in a sun shower.

July 4

Helen Jane McDonald Friel Crosses the North Atlantic at the Age of Five

Starry-eyed dreamer—
daughter of kings, redhead high
as she steps ashore.

July 5

Anisotropic Blues

Will wisdom come as
enantiomeric code
transcribed by the soul?

July 6

What Makes for a Life?

Adrift on acreage?
Anchored in relationships?
What makes for a life?

July 7

Retrieving

Red breasts lament as
she safely ransoms their babe
from her golden one.

July 8

Hypnopompic

Heat lightning, thunder,
and torrent transport senses
to their genesis.

July 9

Antebellum Hearth

Cavernous womb light
and warmth stir ancestral dreams
once etched in the stone.

July 10

Delta Lyrae Conjunction at Dawn

Hypatia weaves her
golden thread through my soul's loom,
endowing wisdom.

July 11

Cicadian Rhythms

Sunlight precesses
to the proud crescendo of
tymbal troubadours.

July 12

South Central Silk Route

Beauty of the morn;
lithe ballerina aloft
as she feeds her brood.

July 13

Mujahid of the Rose Garden

Rotund descendent
of Persian warriors now
guards floral oils.

July 14

Burning Toast As I Rummage Through a Two-Hundred-Year-Old Root Cellar

Relegated to
reptilian brain; how many
futures have you saved?

July 15

Welsh Rabbit

You venture forth from
neighbor Heulyn Owain's hayfield;
Harlech in your heart.

July 16

Of Rainbows and Wren Song

Loved ones, when I join
you, what joy I'll feel! Yet, how
I'll miss my senses.

July 17

Ablutions

Drenched in morning dew,
preening shrouded in pampas—
contently warbling.

July 18

Screened Back

The distant laughter
of factory children liven
mountain memories.

July 19

Protestant Vespers

Methodist bell airs
sweeten the summer skies and
sanctify suppers.

July 20

A Novitiate's Love of an Old Monk
Inspires a New Generation

Ann waxed poetic
about Gregor's peas and set
the course of my life.

July 21

Tag Teamin'

Gentle workers swoop
around me, as in geo
centric precession.

July 22

Forty Years

You ne'r turned your back
on her, your Irish twin, and
she e'er turns her heart.

July 23

Sweltering with Joy

Gathering in the heat;
we celebrated life with
children's water games.

July 24

Bellerophon

Pegasus smitten—
you plummet from the heavens
as Diptera soars.

1   Introduction

1

Our overarching aim is to determine the safety, toler
post-menopausal females with emerging Frontotem
of the disease process.   FTLD, characterized
language and self-regulatory capacities, when fu
dementia in individuals under 65 years of age, re
Onyike]. Recent global epidemiological data from
has a prevalence of between 3 and 26% [Schro
second leading cause of early onset dementia
onset in the   decade of life [1,2,3].   As
developed work   expected to approach 30
United States afo   [Shumaker et al., 2003].
research.
FTLD consists of 3 subtypes; 2 language d
fluent aphasia) and a disorder of behavior
social conduct (e.g., impulsive eating) [Mc
most common form of motor neuron dise
greater prevalence of bulbar onset in fem
              between FTLD and ALS, with t

July 25

Expatriate

Bones, beef, cakes, and ale—
ach, give me my Highland Vale
away from Dis heat!

July 26

Colonial Rule

When clothianidin
grain collapses the chain, who
will be next to reign?

July 27

Brian Francis Escorts His Father Across the Bardo

Malas and rosaries
meld as father and son tone
their ancient verses.

July 28

Base Behavior

Had Hercules lured
Hydra with bromides her blue
mores might have been cured.

July 29

Precious Stones

Macedonians
labor along ancient routes,
laden with peaches.

July 30

Cerulean

Gratitude fills me
For all things—but most of all
for cerulean trees.

July 31

The Rogerian Canine

A score of Summers—
eyes dim, gaits diminish, ebb;
Hearts ever loyal.

August 1

Chance Encounters

As coins in a fount—
the plucking of petals stirs
heart string melodies.

August 2

Tropical Fever

Pre-dawn ethos stirs
Palenque's call: Leave it all
for rain forest puers.

August 3

Sisters of the Sunda Shelf

Scurry and scatter
seeds of our continent's trees
as kin seed the world.

August 4

Prime Real Estate

Freezing and thawing—
fractionation forms landscapes.
Communities thrive.

August 5

Brave Heart

Mom's leery of you.
Why!?! You sing, bearing water
and rues. Watch me fly!

August 6

Blues of My Youth

Sandbox memories—
blue skies, trees, flowers, water
live on in the garden.

August 7

Mid-Summer Transformation

Sublimation heals—
boundaries blurred twixt earth and sky.
Return to the land.

August 8

Empty-Nest Syndrome

Like Giving Trees we
prop doors free; offering seed
for their young to feed.

August 9

Twenty-First-Century Victory Gardens

The secrets of health
like Alexandria's wealth
lie shrouded on Earth.

August 10

Hosta

Regal bearing and
color disguise a robust
child of the forest.

August 11

Black Butterflies

Drab to human eyes
while scintillating in their
ultraviolet world.

August 12

Priestess Murphy

Had Father Murphy
been a woman, might Wexford
have been led lex-ward?

August 13

Comenius

Moravian Star—
pastoral visionary
of mind and spirit.

August 14

Bell's Inequality

Entangled once, now
worlds apart—empaths surpass
Gisin's telepaths.

August 15

Kaleidoscope of the Shadows

Moonlight gives way to
choreographical sway—
shadows in the wind.

August 16

Self-Actualization

She lingers briefly,
Bids Godspeed to the languid;
Then takes to the skies.

August 17

Contrast

A patch of blue robe—
a moth finds its way in fog.
Twilight blankets both.

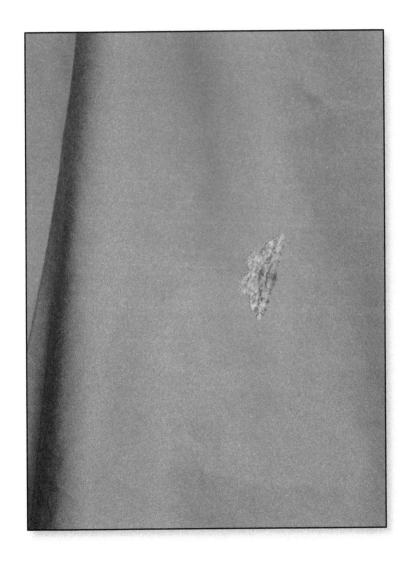

August 18

Rag-Curled Dreamer

Rag curl cloud dreaming—
kite tail strips streaming aloft
drifting toward heaven.

August 19

Thresholds

Sensate awareness;
a strand caresses a hand—
tangeré stirrings.

August 20

Hues

Fleeting sun-showers—
horizons blush scarlet as
light bursts through shadows.

August 21

Of Monarchs and Men

Offspring on the winds—
intergenerational
diasporas thrive.

August 22

Eastern Tiger Swallowtail

Meandering fro—
fecund marshlands his North Star.
She bides in meadows.

August 23

Celestial Herald

An encircled moon—
spices perfume the breezes.
Irene approaches.

August 24

Eileen Mo Mhuirnín

"Mo Mhuirnín" he'd smile
as he tousled the curls of
his darlin' twin girl.

August 25

Thanksgiving

Summer fires blaze—
twin cousins harbinger his
firstborn's arrival.

August 26

Haute Cuisine

Hunters gatherers—
senses refined over time,
heralding culture.

August 27

Brushpile Bungalows

Oak leaf lined hallows—
garden fauna settle in.
Threshold chitterings.

August 28

Nature's Bounty

Sun-dappled coppice—
tantalizing sustenance,
shrouding and shelter.

August 29

Foundations

Rooted in the land—
crown soaring boldly skyward,
branches bridging worlds.

August 30

Red Rubber Boot Reminiscings

A week of rainfall—
dreams of childhood Septembers,
prancing through puddles.

August 31

Winterthur Transitions Through Summer

Snow white to slate blue—
absorbing, transforming copse
reveals passages.

September 1

Diversity

Nadir Summer niche—
hungry babes shedding their down,
Autumn welcomings.

September 2

Chickadee Choreography

Whirling as he sups—
chirping crescendo quickens
as in Dervish chant.

September 3

Spectabilis

Dormant now, coeur spent.
Sigh filled lispings to the wind:
love is behavior.

September 4

Hibiscus

Subtropical blush
sveltely waxing up the coast—
temperate diva.

September 5

Passer domesticus

A score of summers—
speckled progenitor serves
to mentor offspring.

September 6

Pluie Potency

Thunderous labors—
scattered seeds; streams gorged with loam.
Zeus dozes in soft light.

September 7

A-maize-ing

Forty thousand round,
five hundred twenty four million tons—
one billion children.

September 8

Sunrise on the Susquehanna

Wistful kin of yore
illuminate what they no
longer see or feel.

September 9

Cycle of Life

Relentless groundswell—
shifting the anaerobic
aerobic balance.

September 10

Synergism

Daughter of north seas,
Mediterranean son-
navigate as one.

September 11

Evolution

On morn one man sat
amidst mammoth shards, listening—
and that was Adam.

September 12

Full Moon in Pisces

Fairy dust daughter,
delivered by her father—
faith imbues hope, life.

September 13

Stolon Habitat

Leaping into view—
silent protest ensues as
mulch smothers broadleafs.

September 14

Early Morning Rain

Gentle morning rain—
everyone we've ever loved
softly surrounds us.

September 15

Homesteading

Stout oaks vanquish winds.
Stone foundations part waters.
Chimney smoke wafts, curls.

September 16

Night-Light

Guardian of slumber,
sister to all living things—
oaks lull languidly.

September 17

Assurances

Such a lovely word—
gliding off the tongue with grace
while without promise.

September 18

Canyon Cathedral

First light on the cliffs—
joyous chorus of songbirds.
Cobalt river flows.

September 19

If Autumn Never Came

If not for Autumn—
geese would never retrouvaille
awe of chromophores.

September 20

Chickies

Gold-dappled rock face—
songbirds flitting through bowers;
dark waters below.

September 21

Elizabeth Rose

Celtic matriarch—
gentle, patient, tolerant
sage guiding our way.

September 22

Adieu

Gracefully willows
sway their farewells to summer;
winds keening softly.

September 23

Equinox

First light to stardust—
each moment a boundless gift.
Each breath a lifetime.

Mid Life Coda

Born between these signs;
boundless juxtaposition
between sensuality and reason.

* * *

Summer's child, to
dance among dandelions;
living on draughts, cream, and brambleberries.

* * *

Daughter of Autumn
moving through the world une seule;
ever seeking that elusive balance.

About the Author

Claire Flaherty, a lifespan clinical neuropsychologist, whose prior publications have ranged from cognitive neuroscience to humanities, draws her inspiration from the works of W. B. Yeats, Annie Dillard, Mary Oliver, and Matsuo Bashō. As faculty in Penn State Health Neurology, she regularly contributes works of poetry and prose to their literary journal, *Wild Onions.* Dr. Flaherty grew up in New Jersey and spent her childhood summers in the Poconos, where she fell in love with Pennsylvania. She resides in an 1860 farmhouse with her labradoodle Hank. She loves to keep bees and garden, starting plants from seed in her own greenhouse. She practices mindfulness through yoga and tennis. She enjoys photography and astronomy, taking inspiration for her writing from the natural world.

CPSIA information can be obtained
at www.ICGtesting.com
Printed in the USA
LVHW071118100821
695003LV00001B/13